GIANT OCEAN ANIMALS

MANTA RAY

Super Swimmer

BY EMMANUEL MARSHALL

Enslow PUBLISHING

Please visit our website, www.enslow.com. For a free color catalog of all our high-quality books, call toll free 1-800-398-2504 or fax 1-877-980-4454.

Cataloging-in-Publication Data
Names: Marshall, Emmanuel.
Title: Manta ray / Emmanuel Marshall.
Description: Buffalo, NY : Enslow Publishing, 2027. | Series: Giant ocean animals | Includes glossary and index.
Identifiers: ISBN 9781978550711 (pbk.) | ISBN 9781978550728 (library bound) | ISBN 9781978550735 (ebook)
Subjects: LCSH: Mobulidae--Juvenile literature.
Classification: LCC QL638.85.M6 M377 2027 | DDC 597.35--dc23

Published in 2027 by
Enslow Publishing
2544 Clinton Street
Buffalo, NY 14224

Portions of this work were originally authored by Angela Lim and published as *Manta Rays*. All new material in this edition was authored by Emmanuel Marshall.

Cover Designer: Joshua Olson
Interior Designer: Joshua Olson
Editor: Noah Riccardi

Photo Credits: Cover, p. 1 nickeverett1981/Shutterstock.com; pp. 4–5 Carlo Valenzuela/Shutterstock.com; pp. 6–7 crisod/iStockphoto; pp. 8–9 Aryuda View/Shutterstock.com; pp. 10–11, 29 Lewis Burnett/Shutterstock.com; pp. 12–13, 18–19 Global_Pics/iStockphoto; pp. 14–15 Bonish Photography/iStockphoto; pp. 16–17 Katja Tsvetkova/Shutterstock.com; pp. 20–21 RLS Photo/Shutterstock.com; pp. 22–23 lemga/iStockphoto; p. 24 Martin Voeller/iStockphoto; p. 25 isarescheewin/Shutterstock.com; pp. 26–27 Leith Holtzman/Shutterstock.com.

Printed in China

CPSIA compliance information: Batch #QS27ENS: For further information contact Enslow Publishing, at 1-800-398-2504.

TABLE OF CONTENTS

CHAPTER 1

ALL ABOUT MANTA RAYS

Manta rays are fish with flat bodies. Each ray has a large fin on either side of its body. These fins look like wings. Manta rays also have a short, thin tail.

Manta rays are gentle animals.

An adult manta ray can be much larger than a person.

Manta rays flap their fins to swim through the water. They breathe through **gills**. As they swim along, they use these gills to filter **oxygen** out of the water.

TYPES OF MANTA RAYS

There are two main types of manta rays. Giant manta rays are the larger type. They live around the world. Reef manta rays are smaller. They swim in the Indian and Pacific Oceans.

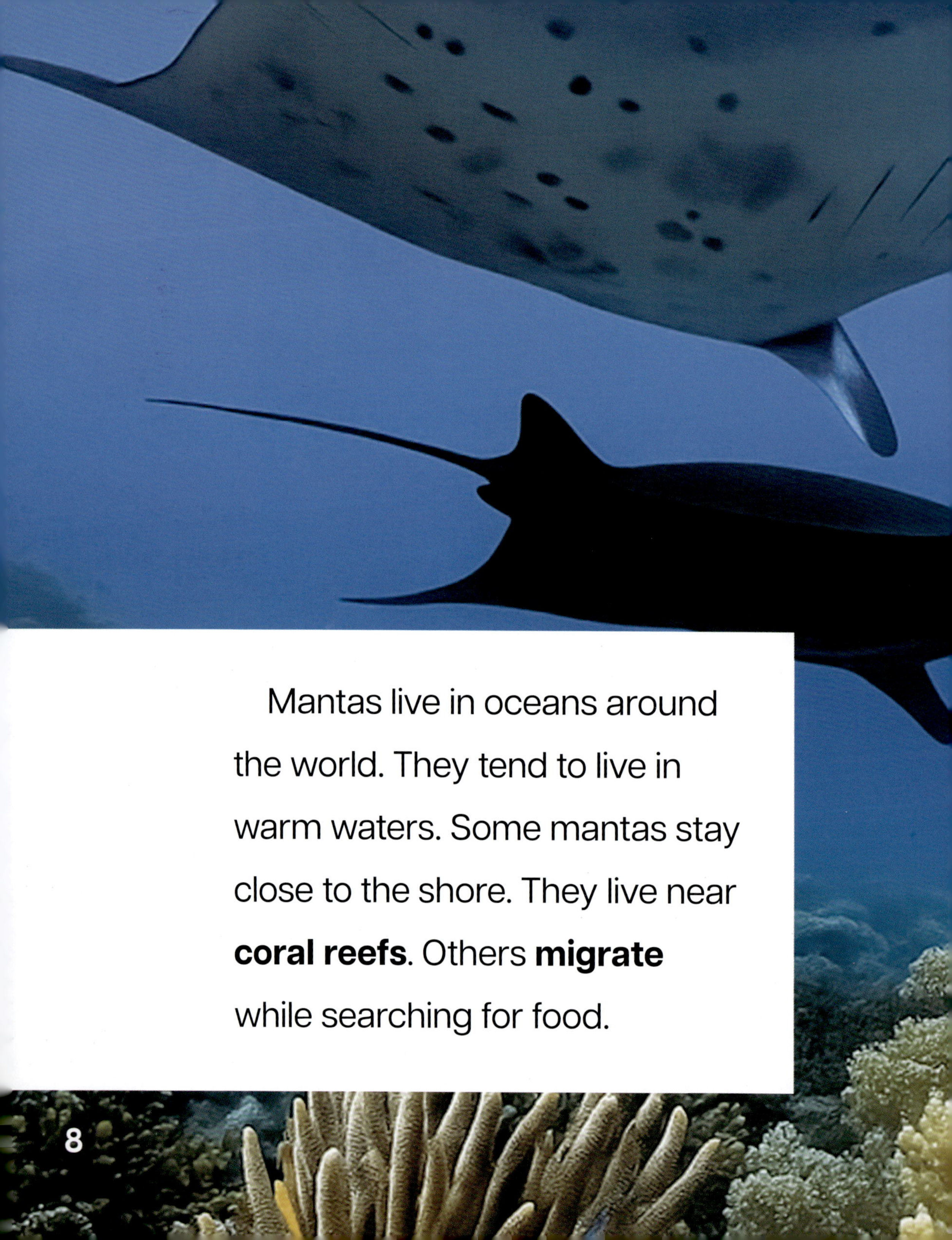

Mantas live in oceans around the world. They tend to live in warm waters. Some mantas stay close to the shore. They live near **coral reefs**. Others **migrate** while searching for food.

Many mantas feed in shallow waters.

Most giant manta rays live in waters near Ecuador.

CHAPTER 2

A MANTA RAY'S BODY

Manta rays' bodies are dark on top. Their bellies can be black or white. Manta rays are related to sharks. Like sharks, they have **cartilage** instead of bones.

A manta ray glides over the ocean floor.

A manta ray's mouth stays open most of the time.

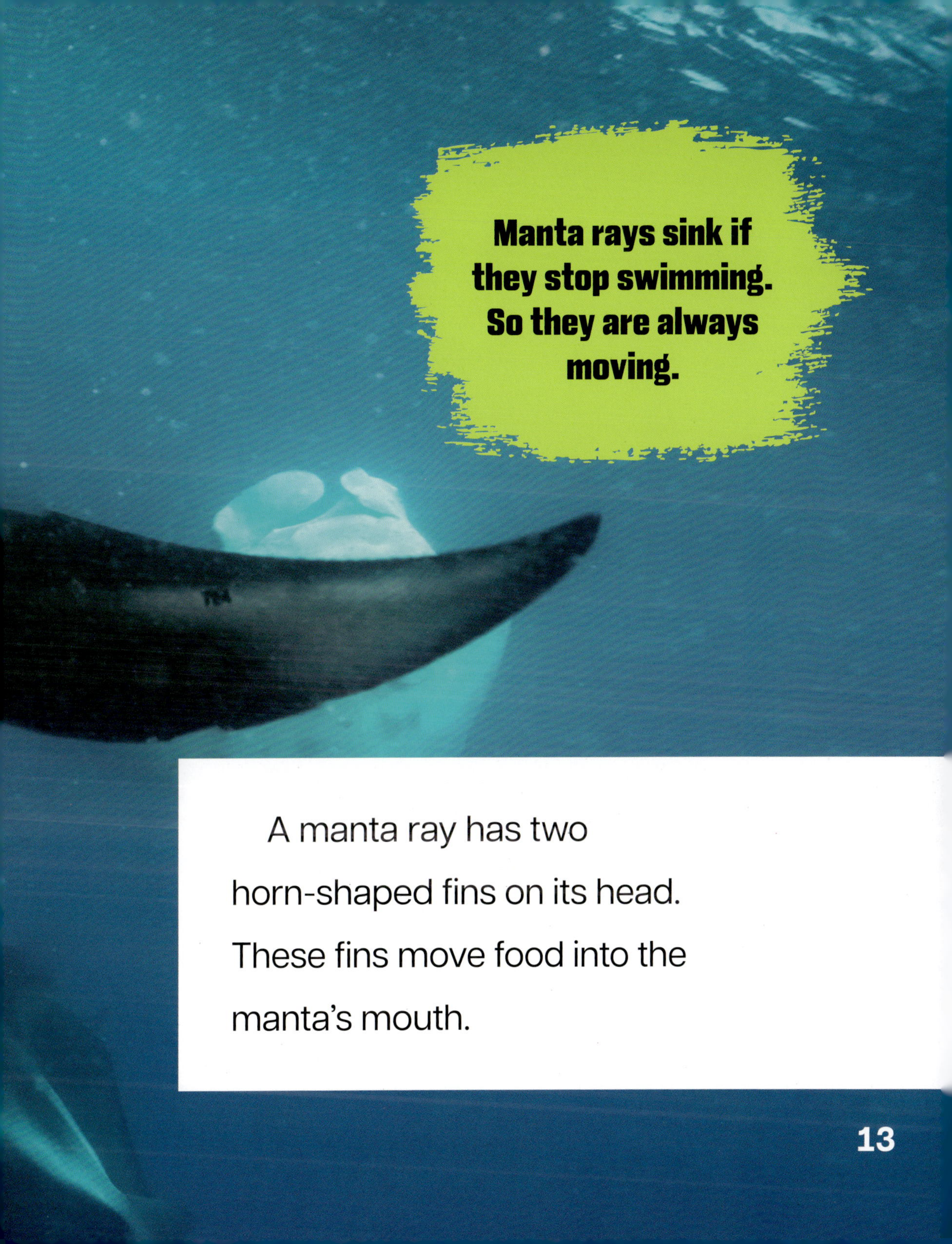

Manta rays sink if they stop swimming. So they are always moving.

A manta ray has two horn-shaped fins on its head. These fins move food into the manta's mouth.

Many kinds of rays can leap up out of the water.

Some manta rays can reach massive sizes. Their fins can spread up to 26 feet (7.9 m) wide. The largest rays can weigh more than 5,000 pounds (2,268 kg).

GENTLE GIANTS

In the past, some people feared manta rays. Stories said mantas jumped up and grabbed people off boats. However, these stories are not true. Manta rays don't harm humans.

CHAPTER 3

FILTER FEEDERS

Manta rays usually swim alone. But they sometimes gather in groups to hunt. They eat tiny sea creatures, such as **plankton** and **krill**.

Manta rays are filter feeders, or animals that suck food out of the water.

Manta rays may flip and roll to scoop up as much food as they can.

Mantas swim with their mouths open. They suck in water and food.

Some manta rays have spots on their bellies. Each manta has its own unique pattern.

BIG BRAINS

Manta rays have the largest brains of any fish. As a result, they are quite smart. They have strong senses. They can even recognize themselves in mirrors.

Sometimes mantas swim quickly together in a circle. The water between them swirls. Krill become trapped in the swirling water. They make an easy meal.

A group of manta rays is called a squadron.

Krill are only about 2 inches (5 cm) long. They float in ocean water.

CHAPTER 4

SAVING MANTA RAYS

Orcas and sharks hunt manta rays. But humans are their biggest **threat**. People fish for manta rays.

Giant manta rays are endangered, which means they are at risk of dying out forever.

People catch mantas for food. They also use parts of mantas as medicine. As a result, some manta ray numbers became very low.

Parts of manta ray gills are used in some medicines.

Many aquariums have manta rays for visitors to see.

Divers can sometimes see mantas up close.

Many countries made manta fishing against the law. Manta **populations** grew back. Higher numbers of mantas also helped bring people to visit those countries.

Manta rays have white spots on their backs. These spots change sizes when mantas greet one another.

LONG LIVES

Manta rays can live for 50 years. But they do not have many babies during their lives. As a result, their populations are especially hurt by fishing.

TEST YOUR KNOWLEDGE

Take this quiz to test your knowledge.

1. Write a sentence that describes the main idea of Chapter 4.

2. Would you want to swim with a manta ray in the wild? Why or why not?

3. What is the biggest threat to manta rays?

- **A.** sharks
- **B.** orcas
- **C.** humans

4. Why does having few babies mean that manta ray populations are especially hurt by hunting?

- **A.** Manta numbers grow back slowly.
- **B.** Mantas have short lifespans.
- **C.** Manta numbers grow back quickly.

5. What does **massive** mean in this book?

Some manta rays can reach ***massive*** *sizes. Their fins can spread up to 26 feet (7.9 m) wide.*

- **A.** very big
- **B.** small
- **C.** unknown

6. What does **swirls** mean in this book?

Sometimes mantas swim quickly together in a circle. The water between them ***swirls****.*

- **A.** warms
- **B.** darkens
- **C.** spins

Answers can be found on page 32.

GLOSSARY

cartilage
Tissue that is softer and more bendable than bone.

coral reefs
Large groups of animals known as corals living in warm, shallow waters. Reefs are mainly built from coral skeletons.

gills
Parts of fish that help them breathe underwater.

krill
Small animals that float in the sea. They look like shrimp.

migrate
To move from one part of the world to another.

oxygen
A gas that animals need to breathe to survive.

plankton
Tiny creatures that often float in big groups in the ocean.

populations
Groups of animals that live in particular places.

threat
Something that is likely to cause danger or harm.

unique
Different from all others.

FOR MORE INFORMATION

BOOKS

Andrews, Elizabeth. *Marine Biome*. Minneapolis, MN: Abdo Publishing, 2022.

Kenney, Karen Latchana. *Coral Reefs*. Minneapolis, MN: Bellwether Media, 2022.

WEBSITES

Britannica Kids: Ray

kids.britannica.com/kids/article/ray/390089

Learn about mantas and other types of rays at this site.

National Geographic Kids: Coral Reef Facts

natgeokids.com/uk/discover/geography/general-geography/coral-reef-facts/

Many manta rays live in coral reefs. Learn about these reefs at this website.

Publisher's note to educators and parents: Our editors have carefully reviewed these websites to ensure that they are suitable for students. Many websites change frequently, however, and we cannot guarantee that a site's future contents will continue to meet our high standards of quality and educational value. Be advised that students should be closely supervised whenever they access the internet.

INDEX

Answer Key:
1. Answers will vary; 2. Answers will vary; 3. C; 4. A; 5. A; 6. C